CANADA'S
WEST COAST

by Chris Cheadle

Canada's
WEST COAST

by Chris Cheadle

Altitude Publishing

The Canadian Rockies / Vancouver

Canada's West Coast

Cataloguing in Publication Data
Cheadle, Chris, 1957-
Canada's West Coast
ISBN 1-55153-202-6
1.Pacific Coaast (B.C.)--pictorial works I.Title
FC3845.P2C43 2002   917.11'1044'0222   C2002-911024-6
F1089.P2C43 2002

Production
Design — Stephen Hutchings
Production assistance — Scott Manktelow, Hermien Schuttenbeld and Kara Turner
Editing — Frances Purslow and Georgina Montgomery
Printed and bound in Canada by Friesen Printers

Altitude GreenTree Program
Altitude will plant twice as many trees as were used in
the manufacturing of this book.

We acknowledge the financial support of the Government of Canada through the
Book Publishing Industry Development Program (BPIDP) for our publishing activities.

Front cover: Tsusiat Falls, West Coast Trail, Vancouver Island
Back cover: Nimpkish memorial burial ground at Alert Bay
Title page: Fiordland Recreation Area. View down Mussel Inlet to Sheep Pass
Frontispiece: A rainforest creek, Juan de Fuca Trail, Vancouver Island
Table of Contents: Aerial view of Pacific Rim National Park, Schooner
Cove and Long Beach

Dedication
Dedicated to my mother, Yvonne, and father, the late Bill Cheadle.

Altitude Publishing
The Canadian Rockies and Vancouver
Head office: 1500 Railway Ave., Canmore, Alberta T1W 1P6
1-800-957-6888 • www.altitudepublishing.com

Map and Essays

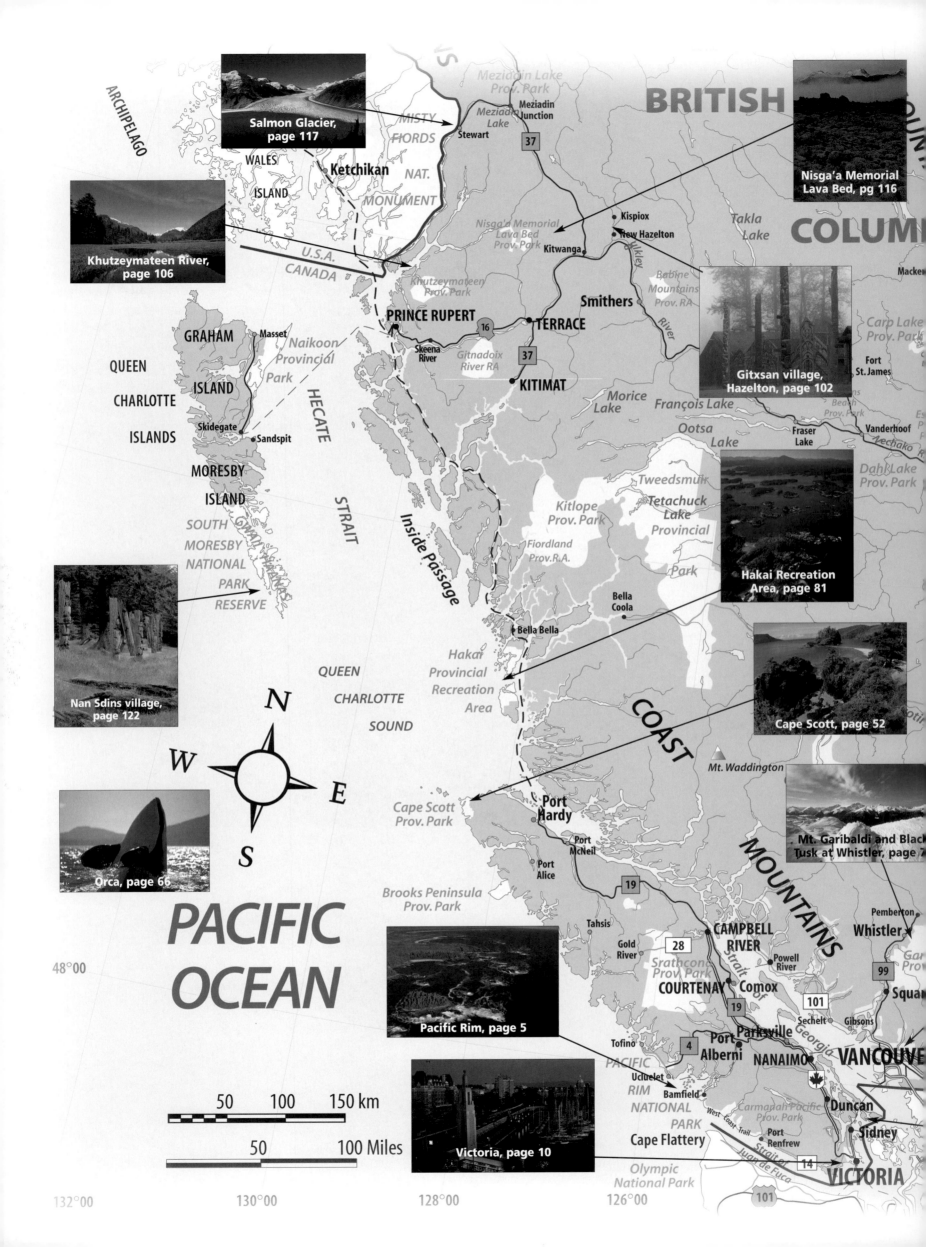

Salmon Glacier, page 117

Nisga'a Memorial Lava Bed, pg 116

Khutzeymateen River, page 106

Gitxsan village, Hazelton, page 102

Nan Sdins village, page 122

Hakai Recreation Area, page 81

Cape Scott, page 52

Orca, page 66

Mt. Garibaldi and Black Tusk at Whistler, page 7

Pacific Rim, page 5

Victoria, page 10

BRITISH

COLUMB

Archipelago

Meziadin Lake Prov. Park

Misty Fiords Nat. Monument

Meziadin Junction

Meziadin Lake

Stewart

37

WALES ISLAND

Ketchikan

Nisga'a Memorial Lava Bed Prov. Park

Kispiox

New Hazelton

Kitwanga

Takla Lake

Carp Lake Prov. Park

U.S.A.
CANADA

Khutzeymateen Prov. Park

Smithers

Babine Mountains Prov. RA

Fort St. James

GRAHAM

Masset

Naikoon Provincial Park

PRINCE RUPERT

16

Skeena River

TERRACE

37

Gitnadoix River RA

QUEEN

CHARLOTTE

ISLAND

KITIMAT

Morice Lake

François Lake

Ootsa Lake

Fraser Lake

Vanderhoof

Nechako

Skidegate

Sandspit

ISLANDS

HECATE

Dahl Lake Prov. Park

MORESBY

ISLAND

Kitlope Prov. Park

Tetachuck Lake Provincial Park

Tweedsmuir

STRAIT

Inside Passage

Fiordland Prov.R.A.

SOUTH MORESBY NATIONAL PARK RESERVE

GWAII HAANAS

Bella Coola

QUEEN

CHARLOTTE

SOUND

Hakai Provincial Recreation Area

Bella Bella

COAST

Mt. Waddington

Pemberton

N
W E
S

Cape Scott Prov. Park

Port Hardy

MOUNTAINS

PACIFIC OCEAN

Port McNeil

Port Alice

19

Whistler

99

Gar Prov

Squar

48°00

Brooks Peninsula Prov. Park

Tahsis

CAMPBELL RIVER

28

Gold River

Strathcona Prov. Park

Powell River

101

Sechelt

Gibsons

COURTENAY

Comox

19

Strait of Georgia

50 100 150 km

50 100 Miles

Tofino

4

PACIFIC RIM NATIONAL PARK

Ucluelet

Bamfield

West Coast Trail

Carmanah Pacific Prov. Park

Port Renfrew

Parksville

Port Alberni

NANAIMO

VANCOUVE

Duncan

Sidney

Cape Flattery

Juan de Fuca

14

VICTORIA

Olympic National Park

101

132°00   130°00   128°00   126°00

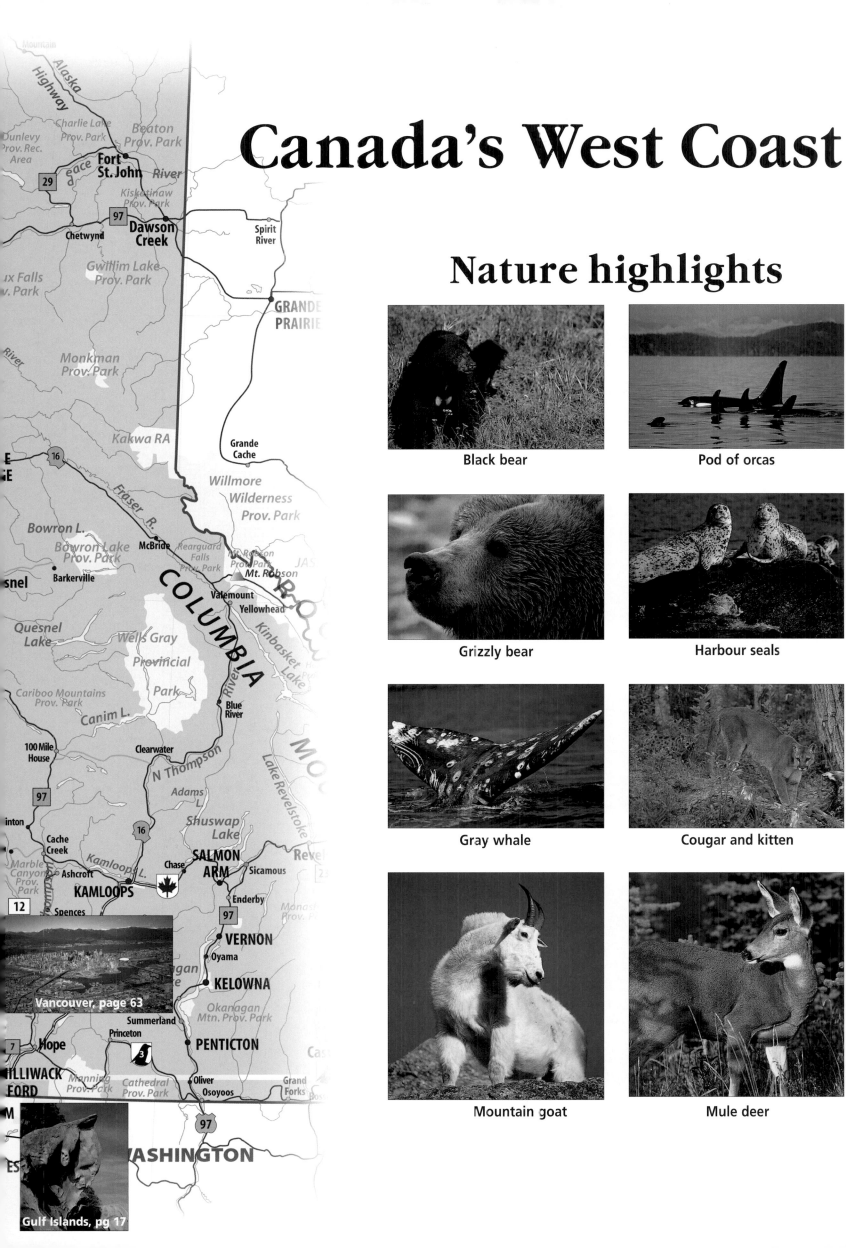

Canada's West Coast

Nature highlights

Black bear

Pod of orcas

Grizzly bear

Harbour seals

Gray whale

Cougar and kitten

Mountain goat

Mule deer

Vancouver, page 63

Gulf Islands, pg 17

Introduction

The shores of the Pacific Northwest hum with a profound energy. The moist Pacific air masses and the plankton-rich ocean currents drive one of the world's most diverse ecosystems. Beneath the roiling waters of the shallows and reefs, forests of swaying kelp host hundreds of species of marine animals.

On shore, the arching canopy of the great rainforest shelters foraging bears, wolves, cougars, elk and deer, while nesting seabirds rest in the mossy branches of 1000-year-old giant spruce, cedar, hemlock and fir. Thousands of rivers and creeks nurture steelhead trout and the five species of Pacific salmon—Chinook, Coho, Sockeye, Chum and Pink.

Ancient seabeds, thrust upward during tectonic collisions, evidence the relentless force of erosion. High above the shore, the jagged mountain peaks and polished rock faces are crowned in snow and ice. They overlook a landscape that carries the scars of glaciation.

As the last Ice Age came to a close about 10,000 years ago, humans gradually arrived in the Pacific Northwest. By the time the first European explorers reached the area, the population of First Nations peoples on the coast was the highest of all aboriginal populations in Canada. Today, First Nations communities of the Pacific Northwest proudly celebrate their heritage with traditional ceremonies, coastal canoe journeys, cultural education programs and the production of sophisticated artwork.

Settlement by Europeans began about 200 years ago, first to support the developing fur trade, and then to establish a colony to protect British interests in the region. Gold seekers brought another wave of settlers. Subsequent logging, mining and fishing industries built the towns and cities, roadways and rail lines that we see today.

To capture the images in this book, I have walked the streams of the rainforests, kayaked to remote beaches, sailed the inlets, explored the islands and listened to the wisdom of First Nations elders. Each of my journeys successively added to my sense of awe in this beautiful coast. Through these photographs, I hope their beauty enthralls you too.

above *Japanese maples and creek in Beacon Hill Park, Victoria*

opposite *Thunderbird Park totem poles and the Empress Hotel, Victoria*

page 10–11 *The legislative buildings and the Empress Hotel face Victoria's Inner Harbour*

The Culture of Nature

For more than a century, visitors have been captivated by Victoria's gentle charms. James Douglas first sailed into this perfect natural harbour, seeking a location for the new northwest headquarters for the Hudson's Bay Company. He proclaimed the place "a perfect Eden." On March 13, 1843, he selected Camosack as the location for the new post—shortly thereafter renamed Fort Victoria—and so Vancouver Island's first European settlement was established at the site of what is today called Bastion Square.

In Victoria's early days, expansive open meadows were shaded by large Garry oaks and arbutus. Violet camas flowers, prized for their onion-like bulbs by the Songhees peoples, swayed in the springtime sun. Today, Victoria is known as the City of Gardens, thanks to the delightfully

benign climate and 150 years of English horticultural traditions. About a thousand hanging flower baskets bloom throughout the city during the summer. More than 1.25 million visitors flock annually to the world-renowned Butchart Gardens, located in a former limestone quarry at Brentwood Bay. Dozens of other excellent plant collections, such as those at the Horticultural Centre of the Pacific and the Abkhazi Garden, can keep garden enthusiasts busy for days. Each February, the city bursts with cherry blossoms, crocuses and daffodils, signaling the beginning of eight months of frost-free days. Throughout summer and fall, Victoria enjoys more days of sunshine than most other Canadian cities.

From Metchosin to the Saanich Peninsula, gently undulating landscapes are punctuated by a number of granite vistas, ideal for scenic day hikes. Mount Douglas and Mount Tolmie both offer sweeping panoramas over the city and straits to distant mountains. Natural public settings abound in Greater Victoria, with urban areas boasting 48 different parks. Beacon Hill Park combines natural meadows with cultivated exotic trees, and freshwater ponds with seaside beaches. The Lochside and Galloping Goose hiking and biking trails wind through urban and rural greenbelts, connecting the Saanich Peninsula to Victoria and the Western Communities.

Skirting the coastline of southern Vancouver Island, the green waters and beaches of crushed white shell or eroded sandstone turn one's mind to thoughts of beach strolls, kayaking junkets and yachting excursions. Dozens of lakes dot the landscape from Sidney to Sooke, ideal for freshwater swimming and bass or trout fishing. Rivers and creeks course their way to the sea. With millions of salmon migrating through the Georgia and Juan de Fuca straits, sport fishing is a popular year-round pursuit.

above *Ross Fountain at The Butchart Gardens near Victoria*

opposite *Flowering dogwood trees grace the banks of the Cowichan River*

above *The distinctive peeling bark of an arbutus tree trunk*

opposite *Arbutus tree on Moresby Island overlooks
Boundary Pass and Washington State's Mt. Baker*

The Gulf Islands

About 100 million years ago, the giant Farallon tectonic plate forced the land mass, or "terrane," of Wrangellia against the western shores of the North American continent. The distinctive mineral-rich mountains of Vancouver Island, the Queen Charlotte Islands and parts of Alaska are what remain of Wrangellia. As time passed, other plates split and divided, bringing the smaller Pacific Rim and then the Crescent terranes from the southwest. Today, these make up the San Juan River area/Pacific Rim and Victoria's Western Communities, respectively. The tectonic forces pressed the sediments and coral remnants of the low-lying sea bed of ancient Wrangellia into the twisted limestone and sandstone hills of the Gulf Islands.

The Gulf Islands should more accurately be called the Strait Islands. Initial surveys by Captain George Vancouver in 1792 mistakenly identified the area as the Gulf of Georgia. Although subsequent corrections were made, the term "Gulf Islands" remains. It refers to all of the more than 200 islands in the strait.

Buffered from the rolling swells and storms of the Pacific Ocean, the islands attract boating enthusiasts, particularly during the drier months. In summer, the warmer tidal waters of the strait entice swimmers to enjoy a refreshing dip off sun-baked beaches. About 30 marine parks can be found throughout the islands, from Sidney Spit and Cabbage Island in the south to Rebecca Spit and Smelt Bay in the north.

Five of the southern Gulf Islands are served by BC Ferries from Swartz Bay. The rural charm of these islands has attracted a large community of renowned artists, craftspeople and musicians. Saltspring Island, with a population of over 10,000, is the most populated of all the Gulf Islands. East of it lie the Pender Islands, with around 2200 residents total, while Mayne and Galiano are home to about 1,000 residents each. The southernmost island, Saturna, has fewer than 400 permanent residents. The smaller Thetis and Kuper islands can be reached by ferry from Chemainus.

Off Nanaimo, 2500 residents inhabit Gabriola Island, site of the naturally carved sandstone ledge at Malaspina Galleries. South of Courtenay are Denman and Hornby islands. Their fine sandy beaches, such as the one at Hornby's Tribune Bay Provincial Park, make them popular vacation spots. Lasqueti and Texada islands are located due east of Hornby, close to the mainland's Sechelt Peninsula. Opposite Campbell River, Cortes and Quadra mark the end point of the drier south coast zone and the re-emergence of the wet rainforest ecosystems.

above *View across Sansum Narrows to Saltspring Island's Mt. Maxwell at daybreak*

opposite *Sandstone shoreline of Tumbo Island, off Saturna Island*

above *One of BC Ferries' "Spirit Class" vessels passing between Saltspring and Moresby islands, with Pender and Saturna islands beyond, to the left*

opposite *The beautiful Calypso, or fairyslipper, orchid graces the sun-dappled fringes of south coast forests*

above *A snowy winter morning at Canoe Cove Marina, near Sidney*

above *A fallen juniper tree frames yachts at dusk,
Cabbage Island Provincial Marine Park*

above *Gulls and a rainbow near Qualicum Bay, Vancouver Island*

opposite *Skookumchuck Narrows Provincial Park
overlooks one of the world's fastest tidal rapids*

page 24 *Intriguing sandstone shoreline at Fords Cove, Hornby Island*

page 25 *Rebecca Spit Provincial Marine Park, Quadra Island*

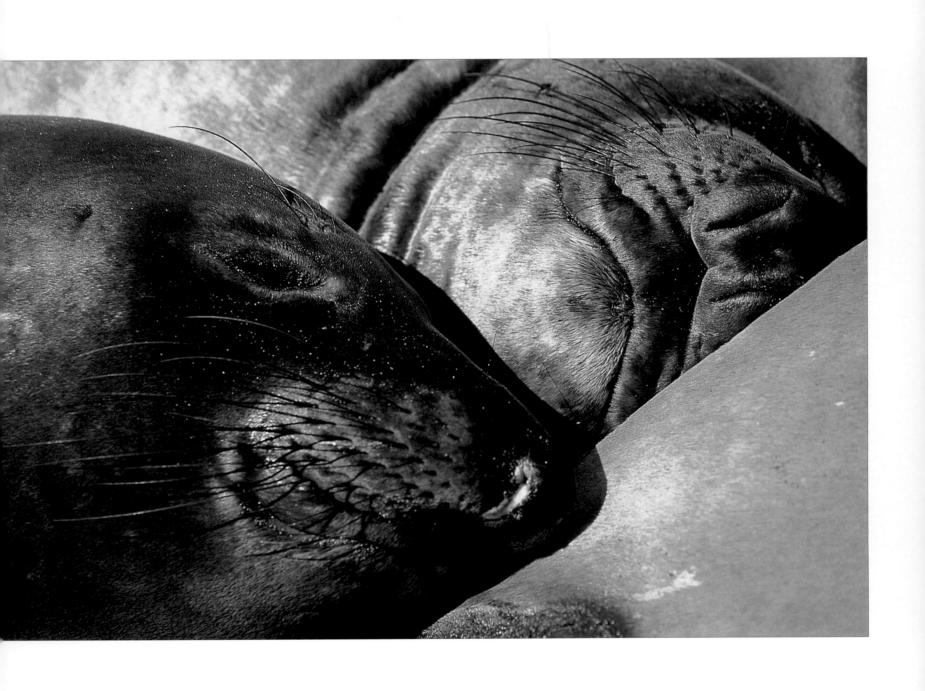

above *Northern elephant seals at rest, Race Rocks Ecological Reserve*

above *Back-lit orcas surface near Saturna Island in the Southern Gulf Islands*

Hiking Forests and Beaches

The spectacular 10-kilometre shoreline trail of East Sooke Regional Park straddles the dry, warm Coastal Douglas-fir biogeoclimatic zone of the inland south coast and the rain-soaked Coastal Western Hemlock zone that typifies the rest of coastal British Columbia. The transition is complete at China Beach, the trailhead for BC Park's newly created Juan de Fuca Marine Trail. The trail extends 47 kilometres north along the strait to the fascinating tide pools of Botanical Beach near Port Renfrew. The West Coast Road provides access to Sombrio Beach, Loss Creek and other trails, but hikers should be fit and well versed in wilderness survival if they plan on embarking far along these routes.

Across the San Juan River from Port Renfrew sits the south entrance to the 77-kilometre West Coast Trail, part of Pacific Rim National Park. From May through September, hikers from around the world test their stamina on the five- to seven-day route. The steep ladders, mucky trails and soft sand beaches make a high level of fitness and excellent footwear vital for anyone attempting the hike. The beach where Tsusiat Falls spills down from the forest is considered by some to be the prettiest spot on the West Coast Trail. Mossy boardwalks wind through towering stands of Sitka spruce and cedar, fern-draped grottos and verdant under-growth. Hikers must also cross the mouths of numerous watercourses, some by foot and some by cable car.

Visible from shore, sea lions, seals, orcas and gray whales feed in the rich Pacific waters. The trail was originally built almost a century ago to aid the rescue of shipwreck survivors along the rough coast (once dubbed the "graveyard of the Pacific"). Artifacts of this heritage—anchors, rusted ship hulls, old logging gear and survival shacks—remain along the trail today.

Another wonderful hiking experience is that offered by the Carmanah Valley, home to what is thought to be the tallest Sitka spruce in the world and the tallest tree in Canada—the Carmanah Giant, standing 95.8 metres high. Caramanah-Walbran Provincial Park, with its groves of Sitka spruce, western hemlock and western redcedar was established thanks to the environmental efforts of many British Columbians. The park is accessed along active logging roads past Nitinat Lake. The park trails end at Stoltmann Grove, which was named for the late Randy Stoltmann, whose photographs were instrumental in drawing attention to environmental issues in the area.

above *Waterfall spilling onto Mystic Beach, Juan de Fuca Trail*

opposite *Botanical Beach tidepools along the Juan de Fuca Trail, near Port Renfrew*

above *Giant Sitka spruce trees thrive in the rainforests of the Carmanah–Walbran Provincial Park*

above *The towering "Three Sisters" in the Carmanah Valley*

above *Sticky cinquefoil blooms on the rocky shores near Pachena Point, West Coast Trail*

opposite *Twilight at Tsusiat Falls, West Coast Trail*

page 34 *Tsocowis Creek, West Coast Trail*

page 35 *Cedar boardwalk and verdant ground cover, West Coast Trail*

above *Orange Juice Creek framed by fresh green needles in a spruce forest, West Coast Trail*

Pacific Wilds

While British Columbia's coastline stretches for more than 27,000 kilometres, the only open Pacific beaches and shoreline accessible by paved public highway north of Port Renfrew are found between Ucluelet and Tofino. Pacific Rim National Park, between Chesterman Beach near Tofino and Florencia Bay to the south, features sweeping, sand beaches. Tidal pools at the base of rocky headlands teem with sea creatures, to the delight of young and old. The diverse inlets, islands, mud flats and exposed beaches of Clayoquot Sound near Tofino were designated a UNESCO biosphere reserve in 2000.

At Amphitrite Point lighthouse in Ucluelet, the newly created Wild Pacific Trail offers stunning vistas of the sea. The harbour is the gateway to Barkley Sound and the Broken Group Islands. This wonderful kayaking and yachting haven of more than 100 islands enables boaters to ease their way from the sheltered inside islands to the wave-buffeted shores favoured by colonies of sea lions and pods of gray whales. The M.V. *Lady Rose*, operating out of Port Alberni, drops off paddling groups at a float at Gibraltar Island. This ship also stops at Bamfield, a historic boardwalk community that serves as the other main departure point to Barkley Sound. Salmon returning to the Stamp-Somass River system attract sport fishers here throughout the summer.

Intrepid mariners who venture beyond Hot Springs Cove and its soothing mineral waters must skirt the treacherous shallows off Estevan Point to reach historic Nootka Sound. The face of the sea has not changed since Captain James Cook and Chief Maquinna first met in 1778. Nuu-chah-nulth legends give credence to the theory that Sir Francis Drake visited the west coast of British Columbia in 1579.

The Nuu-chah-nulth people of this south coast region once ranged along the West Coast from the Brooks Peninsula to Jordan River, and were related to the Makah from Washington state's Olympic Peninsula. They traditionally braved the tempestuous coastal waters in cedar canoes. Armed with mussel-shell-tipped harpoons and seal skin floats, they hunted whales and other sea mammals. Numbering about 28,000 in Cook's time, the Nuu-chah-nulth saw their population plummet below 2000 in the 1930s. Today that number has increased to more than 6000 members.

above *Ahous Bay sunset, Vargas Island, Clayoquot Sound*

above *Combers Beach, Green Point and Long Beach,*
Pacific Rim National Park Reserve

opposite *Lennard Island lighthouse, Chesterman's Beach*
and Meares Island, near Tofino

page 40 *Salal growing from a weathered log, Vargas Island*

page 41 *Low tide at MacKenzie Beach, Tofino*

above *Misty sunrise over small island, Nootka Sound*

opposite *Whaler Islets, Clayoquot Sound*

above *Migrating sandpipers at Grice Bay, Clayoquot Sound*

opposite *Macro view of peat moss*

above *Waves crashing on the rocky shoreline, Nootka Sound*

opposite *Steller's sea lion, Barkley Sound,
Pacific Rim National Park Reserve*

above *Waves crash onto a sandy beach,
Whaler Islets, Clayoquot Sound*

opposite *The western trillium, whose blossom
turns pink to magenta as they age*

above *Sea lions sunning on rocks*

opposite *San Josef Bay, Cape Scott Provincial Park*

above *Rugged shoreline of Catala Island, Esperanza Inlet*

opposite *Ochre sea stars, leaf barnacles, feather boa kelp,
coralline algae and eel-grass*

above *Cape Scott at the northwest tip of Vancouver Island*

opposite *Japanese glass fishing float at San Josef Bay,*
Cape Scott Provincial Park

Strathcona Provincial Park

Stretching from sea level at Herbert Inlet on the west coast of Vancouver Island to high rocky summits, Strathcona Provincial Park contains six of the seven tallest peaks on the island. A series of volcanic eruptions more than 350 million years ago began building these peaks on the floor of the Pacific Ocean. Gradually, this submerged mountain system was exposed, forming the backbone of the island.

Strathcona's rugged wilderness is home to wolves, bears, cougar, deer, Roosevelt elk and the endangered Vancouver Island marmot. Visitors to British Columbia's oldest provincial park may also spot the chestnut-backed chickadee, red-breasted nuthatch, winter wren, kinglet, gray jay, Steller's jay or band-tailed pigeon. As well, the park supports numerous blue grouse, ruffed grouse and a limited number of unique Vancouver Island white-tailed ptarmigan.

The valleys and mountains are criss-crossed by an extensive network of trails. Hikers typically access the park by road from the Mt. Washington ski area or inland from Campbell River. For novice backpackers, trips into the relatively flat Forbidden Plateau Recreation Area, adjacent to the Mt. Washington ski resort, provide a fulfilling taste of the beautiful alpine setting. Well-established trails weave through a landscape of trout-filled alpine lakes that reflect the rocky peaks of Strathcona Park. Forbidden Plateau takes its name from a Comox First Nations legend that tells of women and children who, after being sent there for safety during a battle between the Comox and a neighbouring aboriginal group, disappeared without a trace. Because it was believed they were eaten by evil spirits, travel to the area was subsequently forbidden.

More adventurous hikers who are prepared for some steep climbing can access the ridges above the plateau and enjoy sweeping vistas from mountains such as Albert Edward, Castlecrag and Jutland. Farther north, in the centre of Strathcona Park, climbers can tackle the island's highest peak, the Golden Hinde, standing 2195 metres above sea level. A 16-kilometre hike to Della Falls, Canada's highest free-falling waterfall, can be reached from the western end of Great Central Lake near Port Alberni.

above *Cream Lake and Mt. Septimus, Strathcona Provincial Park*

opposite *Golden Hinde (rt), the tallest peak on Vancouver Island, in Strathcona Provincial Park*

above *Spotted owl near Bedwell River*

above *Bunchberry blossoms and fern*

Milltown to Metropolis

Below the ice-capped North Shore mountains, Vancouver's steel and glass towers glisten. British Columbia's commercial centre was Canada's fastest-growing city throughout the 20th century. Today the growth continues, with the Greater Vancouver region nearing 1.9 million people. Each year, more than 3000 ships enter Burrard Inlet, the busiest harbour in the country. Cruise ships, float planes and all manner of pleasure and commercial vessels share the busy waters. To the south, the shores of the Fraser River are home to canneries, sawmills and tugboat operators. The river's extensive, nutrient-rich flood plain provides fertile land for the bountiful farms throughout the delta and the Fraser Valley.

The first Europeans settled in the Vancouver area in 1827, when the Hudson's Bay Company

established the fur-trading post of Fort Langley, 48 kilometres up the Fraser River. The Cariboo gold rush that began in 1858 enticed more than 25,000 people up the Fraser River. Pioneering trails to the gold fields from the lower mainland opened up the province's interior. In 1859, the colony of British Columbia was born, with New Westminster as its capital.

Not far from New Westminster, the abundant Douglas-fir and cedar forests on the shores of Burrard Inlet seemed an ideal location for Edward Stamp to locate his sawmill operation in 1867. The colourful "Gassy" Jack Deighton opened a saloon nearby to serve the mill hands. The little logging town of Gastown was officially renamed Granville in 1870. The obvious merits of the deep natural harbour at Burrard Inlet encouraged the Canadian Pacific Railway to locate its western terminus nearby, and in 1886 the City of Vancouver was incorporated.

Over the past century, Vancouver has evolved from a western resource town to a well-known international destination. A wide cross-section of European and Asian immigrants has enhanced the cosmopolitan flavour of the city with a multitude of specialty shops and customs. High-tech firms and movie studios now share the stage with the resource sector. The once industrial waterfront of False Creek has been revitalized with parks, modern housing complexes, Granville Island Market, marinas and a seaside promenade. Beautiful beaches, such as Jericho and Kitsilano, extend from the University of British Columbia campus along the south shores of Burrard Inlet to the 10-kilometre seawall at Stanley Park. The park is a preserve of old-growth forest amid gardens, fields and ponds, and is home to the Vancouver Aquarium.

above *Downtown Vancouver, looking along Cambie Street*

above *Aerial view of False Creek, downtown Vancouver,
Stanley Park, Burrard Inlet and the North Shore*

pages 64-65 *Twilight vista from Grouse Mountain Ski Resort*

above *An orca spyhopping in Georgia Strait*

above *Spanish Banks, at the southern entrance to Burrard Inlet*

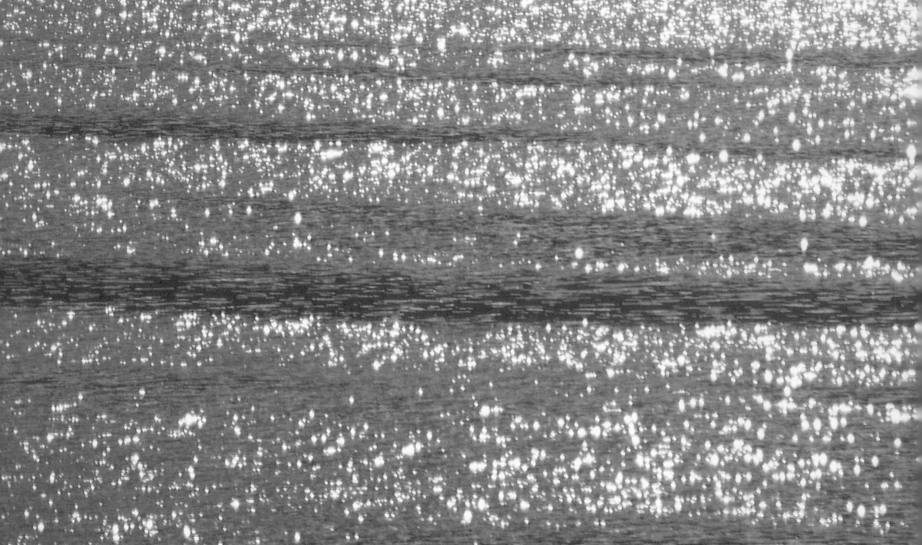

above *Great blue heron, George C. Reifel Migratory Bird Sanctuary, Fraser River delta*

opposite *Gillnetting fish boat near the mouth of the Fraser River*

Sea to Sky

I t was gold that first opened up the region between Howe Sound and Squamish to European settlers. Pemberton, the first pioneer community established in the area, was originally a waypoint along the earliest overland route to the gold fields, up the Lillooet River. As interior settlement grew, the rough-hewn Pemberton Trail was completed in 1877, linking Lillooet to North Vancouver. Squamish was established as the trailhead and later became the rail terminus for the first stage of the Pacific Great Eastern Railway. This increased accessibility allowed visitors to discover the natural wonders of the Squamish, Whistler and Pemberton valleys. Rainbow Lodge, established on Alta Lake in the Cheakamus Valley in 1914, became British Columbia's premier summer resort.

When roads penetrated the area, including the Sea to Sky Highway, skiers followed—by the millions. Despite what some skeptics had to say about the plan, Whistler Mountain's developers installed the first lifts at the base of the mountain in 1966. Neighbouring Blackcomb Mountain opened in 1978. Today, Intrawest Resorts manages the two facilities, with a staff of about 4000. The operation includes more than 30 lifts that lead to about 200 runs. Whistler-Blackcomb—with the longest fall line and vertical runs of any ski centre on the continent—is consistently voted North America's premier ski resort in industry polls. Stunning 360-degree snow-capped vistas await skiers who ride to the peaks.

European-style Whistler Village, built at the base of both mountains, has become the lively restaurant, nightlife, accommodation and shopping core of the resort. And the fun is not limited to the winter months. A network of paved paths allows cyclists and in-line skaters to wind around the five valley lakes. Mountain biking, golf, tennis, swimming, skateboarding, alpine hiking, river rafting, fishing and even mid-summer skiing and snowboarding give visitors a reason to enjoy this mountain community year round.

At Squamish, the Stawamus Chief, a polished granite monolith, attracts more than 160,000 climbers annually to its 180 rock-climbing routes. Emerging through the glaciers of the last Ice Age, Mt. Garibaldi today beckons backpackers to test their stamina on the scenic trails that weave through Garibaldi Provincial Park. The prolific salmon and steelhead runs up the Squamish and Cheakamus rivers draw anglers and eagles by the thousands. During the Brackendale Winter Eagle Festival in late December, over 1000 eagles a day may be seen lining the riverbanks.

above *Highway 99 on Howe Sound, looking north to Tantalus Range*

opposite *Whistler Village promenade*

above *View to Mt. Garibaldi and Black Tusk,*
from the peak of Whistler in winter

opposite *Whistler Mountain meadow in summer*

Northwest Coast Traditions

Complex art forms of the First Nations cultures of the Northwest Coast reveal themselves in totem poles, masks, costumes, prints, carvings and exquisite jewellery. The stories and crests depicted in aboriginal art are hereditary properties passed on through generations. Animals symbolize important characteristics. The eagle, for example, represents power, wisdom and leadership. The raven, a trickster and transformer, is revered and often the centre of creation mythology. Wolves, bears, orcas, halibut, salmon, frogs, bumblebees, loons, herons and hummingbirds are all portrayed in various ways by different First Nations groups.

The totem pole era reached its height in the years immediately following European contact, although the tradition of carving them existed before that. The personal wealth acquired by fur-trading chiefdoms, as well as the availability of steel woodcarving tools, stimulated much of the production of the great totem poles of the 19th century. However, the influence of Christian missionaries, together with a decline in aboriginal populations (a result of numerous epidemics brought by the newcomers), nearly led to the disappearance of the totem pole from coastal Native communities. The removal of many poles to museum collections around the world further thinned the number along the coast.

Family was critical to the culture of aboriginal Northwest Coast societies. The large cedar-plank post-and-beam houses were occupied by extended kinship groups, and reflected the rank and history of each family. Prescribed harvesting areas and salmon streams were owned by particular families. The potlatch ceremony, long misunderstood by outsiders, remains an elaborate form of cultural expression practised by most First Nations of the north coast. It serves to reinforce social status and wealth through the giving of gifts, a process that redistributes goods within the community. The potlatch, which features speeches, dance rituals, feasting and the honouring of guests, celebrates such occasions as memorial services, house- or pole-raising, marriages and hereditary transfers.

The profound changes experienced by Northwest Coast societies following European contact threatened the survival and health of many of the cultures. In recent years, as First Nations populations recover, the repatriation of artefacts from world collections and the teaching of aboriginal languages and customs are fostering a renewed spirit of cultural identity and pride.

above *Kwakwaka'wakw Spirit Bird mask by Randy Bell*

opposite *Hunt Family Dancers with ceremonial regalia*

above *Halibut and fisherman totem, 'Namgis burial ground, Alert Bay*

opposite *Mt. Waddington in the Coast Mountains*

Central Coast Waterways

Cape Caution, Storm Islands, Sorrow Islands, Grief Point and Terror Point are just a few of the place names along British Columbia's outer coast that serve as reminders to mariners of the perils imposed by these lonely shores.

Northbound vessels, including the ferries leaving Port Hardy, must face 65 kilometres of exposed passage at the southern end of Queen Charlotte Sound. The annals of nautical lore brim with harrowing tales of swamped decks and punishing seas—and the tragic results occasionally associated with these. The open seas in this area can build towering swells, with winds sometimes reaching hurricane force. Sub-sea shallows and headlands funnel sweeping currents right into swells, churning the sea into a watery maelstrom. Fortunately, modern weather

reporting and skillful seamanship reduce the risks posed by such a menace. Nonetheless, mariners are relieved to see Cape Calvert to their port side as they approach Safety Cove, on the leeward shores of Calvert Island. For most, the remainder of the journey north is along the sheltered Inside Passage waterway to Prince Rupert.

This marine highway not only serves the British Columbia coast, but also connects Alaska to Puget Sound in Washington. Alaskan and BC ferries share the shipping lanes with giant cruise ships, freighters, tugboats, barges, fishing boats, private yachts and kayaks. Although sheltered from the offshore weather, these waters have strong currents and narrow channels that demand attentive seamanship. Aside from Bella Bella/Waglisla, Shearwater and a few other First Nations villages along the route, the steep forested shores and river valleys along this coast are uninhabited. These islands and inlets are home to the white- or cream-coloured Kermode, or spirit, bear. This unusual genetic variant of the black bear is found only near this coast. An abundance of grizzlies and black bears, wolves, Pacific white-sided dolphins, eagles and osprey inhabit the untarnished wilderness surrounding the Inside Passage.

Many deep fiords reach inland through the Coast Range to pristine estuaries. Nakwakto Rapids, at the entrance to Seymour and Belize inlets, hustles the sea through the narrows at upwards of 30 kilometres per hour, making it the fastest tidal channel in the world. Hakai Recreation Area, on the exposed western shores near Waglisla, is the largest marine park in the province. It offers opportunities for excellent salmon fishing, wilderness yachting and sea kayaking excursions.

above *Pulteney Point lighthouse on Malcolm Island marks the junction of Broughton Strait and Queen Charlotte Sound*

above *The beautiful beaches of Cape Caution in Queen Charlotte Sound, just north of Vancouver Island*

page 80 *Nakwakto Rapids, at the entrance to Seymour and Belize inlets, surge at a peak rate of 30 kilometres per hour, the fastest tidal channel on the coast*

page 81 *Hakai Recreation Area is British Columbia's largest marine park*

Great Bear Rainforest

More than 80 unlogged watersheds along British Columbia's central and northern coast interconnect to form one contiguous region called the Great Bear Rainforest. Biologists consider the area—which is the largest intact coastal temperate rainforest remaining in the world—to be vital to the future of the large mammals that live there. Adventurous travellers who sail into the pristine inlets of the area witness a true wilderness. The estuaries, where marine and terrestrial environments converge at river mouths, are home to a complex web of life.

In springtime, marine mammals such as whales, dolphins, seals and sea lions gorge on the spawning herring and eulachon. During the summer and autumn, salmon return to their birthplace in the rivers along this coast. Bears and wolves drag the protein-rich salmon ashore; leaving the remains to nourish the forest soils. The preservation of this unfragmented and complete ecosystem is the goal of the Raincoast Conservation Society and others.

Fiordland Recreation Area is a 91,000-hectare habitat preserve which lies at the core of the Great Bear Rainforest, north of Waglisla. The fiords, carved by glaciers, rise steeply to over 1000 metres on either side of Mussel and Kynoch inlets. On precariously narrow ledges, sure-footed mountain goats graze contentedly. Red ochre petroglyphs etched on polished rock faces portray traditional hunting territories of the Kitasoo/Xaixais First Nation. Spectacular waterfalls cascade into the sea, while snow-capped peaks of the Coast Mountains gleam above the dense forests of the valleys. The area is accessible only by boat or float plane.

Large mammals require extensive ranges well beyond the Fiordland Recreation Area if their long-term survival is to be ensured. Environmental groups and coastal First Nations organizations sponsor scientific research to inform the public and lobby governments about issues affecting the rich and unique natural heritage of this region.

above *Eco-touring vessel* Duen *in Poison Cove, adjacent to Mussel Inlet*

opposite *Mussel Inlet estuary, Fiordland Recreation Area*

above *Grizzly bear feeding on pink salmon near Knight Inlet Lodge*

opposite *Pink salmon migrating upstream to spawn*

above *Tamahi River after a winter snowfall*

opposite *Waterfall at Oatswish Bay, central coast*

above *Aerial view of Kynoch Inlet and waterfall*

opposite *Paddlers approach Kynoch Falls, Fiordland Recreation Area*

above *Pristine spring greenery in James Bay, Pooley Island*

opposite *Bald eagle*

above *Khutze Inlet estuary, opposite Princess Royal Island, Inside Passage*

opposite *Lupines and sedges in Culpepper Lagoon estuary, Fiordland Recreation Area*

pages 94-95 *Lard Creek flows out to Culpepper Lagoon, on the central coast*

Shifting Human Tides

First Nations villages and harvesting camps were once prolific along the coast of the Inside Passage, all the way to Prince Rupert. Today, no major settlements remain, and there are fewer inhabitants in the area than when European explorers initially arrived. Waglisla, now the largest village along this part of the coast, is home to 1200 members of the Heiltsuk First Nation, formerly known as the Bella Bella.

Butedale, once the site of a busy salmon cannery, sits on the east shores of Princess Royal Island. The decaying, mossy remains of the community reflect the fate of most of the 223 cannery operations established on the west coast during the first half of the 20th century. In 1867, James Syme opened British Columbia's first commercial cannery, situating it on the Fraser River across from New Westminster. So began the era of large-scale commercial fishing in the province. Because of the lack of refrigeration technology, "on-location" company canneries rapidly spread along the coast, springing up in remote inlets close to the rich fishing grounds. In Port Edward, south of Prince Rupert, North Pacific Cannery Village welcomes visitors to see displays of restored canning facilities in this once-thriving operation.

Early logging operators, who supplied wood to the canneries and other markets, also established their presence in the isolated inlets. With the coastal forests growing down to the edge of the steep-sided shorelines, loggers were able to slide felled trees to the sea and float them out. Many independent logging outfits towed floating camps from one area to another, harvesting the seemingly endless supply of timber. As the 20th century progressed, several logging enterprises consolidated into a few large companies. Advances in logging technology using rail- and road-harvesting techniques eventually prompted the establishment of land-based logging camps and the demise of the itinerant float camps.

above *The waters of the Inside Passage south of Prince Rupert are illuminated by celestial beams of light*

opposite *Butedale, once a thriving salmon cannery community, Princess Royal Island*

above *The Lawyer Islands at sunset, just south of Prince Rupert*

above *Tugboat tows a mobile camp through the misty channels of the Inside Passage*

Skeena, River of Mists

PInhabited along its lower reaches by the coastal Tsimshian people, and beyond Kitselas Canyon by the related Gitxsan, the Skeena River has long rivaled the Fraser for its significant runs of salmon and steelhead. Not until the 1860s, however, did the river garner much attention from non-aboriginals. Captain Vancouver's early voyage of discovery in 1793 failed to mention the 621-kilometre river. In 1864, Captain Tom Coffin steamed the first paddlewheeler past the shifting bars of the lower Skeena, making it as far as Terrace. He was carrying supplies for the Collins Overland Telegraph Company, which was attempting to connect San Francisco to Europe via British Columbia. This venture was later aborted at Telegraph Creek on the Stikine River, because of the advent of undersea cables. Regular steamer service on

the Skeena began in 1891, when the Caledonia, owned by the Hudson's Bay Company, plied 288 kilometres inland to Hazelton, located at the confluence of the Skeena and Bulkley rivers.

Totem poles and communal houses preside over the reconstructed Gitxsan village of 'Ksan, on the 7000-year-old site at Hazelton. The Wet'suwet'en, an Athabascan-speaking group from up the Bulkley River drainage, have shared the region at Hazelton with the Gitxsan since 1820, when a large rock blocked the salmon run at Hagwilget Canyon. Enterprising First Nations peoples spanned the canyon using remnants of materials employed for telegraph construction. A modern suspension bridge now connects the community with Hazelton. Some of the oldest standing totem poles in British Columbia can still be found at the nearby villages of Kispiox, Kitwanga and Kitwancool. They reflect Gitxsan family heritage and history.

Prince Rupert, a modern city at the Skeena's mouth, is the transportation hub for the north coast. It boasts modern shipping facilities for handling grain, coal and lumber. It is also the terminus for BC Rail and the Yellowhead Highway, for BC Ferries' routes to Vancouver Island and the Queen Charlotte Islands, and for Alaska State Ferries' routes. As well, since the establishment of the first canneries here in the late 1800s, Prince Rupert has been home to the north coast fishing fleet. The Canadian Fishing Company cannery located in Prince Rupert today is the largest such plant in the world. Sport fishing charters routinely return with limit catches of halibut or salmon. Nearby, the Museum of Northern British Columbia has artifacts and exhibits that portray important developments in the area's history.

above *Prince Rupert waterfront at Cow Bay*

above *Skeena River looking north to the Hazelton Mountains*

page 102 *'Ksan, a reconstructed Gitxsan village at Hazelton*

page 103 *Hagwilget Canyon, near the confluence of the Bulkley and Skeena rivers*

above *Fallen totem at Kitwanga (also known as Gitwangak)*

opposite *A few of the traditional Gitxsan totem poles at Gitanyow (Kitwancool)*

Khutzeymateen

The 400-kilometre stretch of land from Knight Inlet to Alaska is a stronghold for grizzly bear populations. An estimated 10,000 to 13,000 bears inhabit British Columbia and the largely undeveloped watersheds on the western slope. The coastal bears, fattened on a diet of salmon, sedge grasses and berries, can reach 455 kilograms. While females limit their range to a few familiar watersheds, the males roam over larger areas.

In spring, the bears head to the estuaries to graze on the sedge grasses and flower bulbs that cover the silty flats. Mothers and cubs keep a wary nose up for the mature males, who pursue mates aggressively at this time. As salmon return to the rivers in summer and autumn, the grizzlies spend their days wandering along the river and fishing in pools. It is not uncommon for them to

expertly strip apart a whole fish and delicately dine on the roe, discarding much of the carcass.

In 1994, the Khutzeymateen Grizzly Bear Sanctuary was established 40 kilometres northeast of Prince Rupert. The sanctuary, also known as K'tzim-a-deen, the Tsimshian word meaning "sheltered place of fish and bears," protects a wilderness watershed of 443 square kilometres. The area supports approximately 50 grizzlies, one of the highest concentrations on the coast. Together, BC Parks and the Tsimshian First Nation manage the reserve, focussing on maintaining its ecological integrity. While controlled viewing of the estuary is permitted, human activity within the area is not encouraged. Visitors may enter the river's mouth only as guests of a select few charter operators who are sanctioned by BC Parks. Mariners who enter the inlet are restricted to outer sections. At the southern extent of the coastal grizzly range at Knight Inlet, visitors may experience a guided bear-viewing excursion while staying at the floating lodge.

From Knight Inlet northwards, the Raincoast Conservation Society is involved in protecting grizzly bear habitat. The group is researching the behaviour and distribution of such key species as grizzly bears and wolves along their coastal range. The impact that hunting and industrial logging may be having on the continued health of these populations is of serious concern to many conservationists.

above *Khutzeymateen River estuary in early June*

opposite *Young Khutzeymateen grizzly feeding on a springtime diet of sedges*

above *Lone paddler glides through the Khutzeymateen Inlet*

above *Khutzeymateen sunset*

above *St. Paul's Anglican church in Gitwangak*

Nisga'a

The Nisga'a First Nation currently occupies four villages near the southern end of the Nass River. At the head of the bay is Gingolx (Kincolith), which began as an Anglican settlement for Nisga'a converts. At the mouth of the river is Laxqalts'ap (Greenville), a traditional eulachon fishing location. Upriver is Gitwinksihlkw (Canyon City), which until 1995, was accessible only by boat or a pedestrian suspension bridge.

In the mid-1700s, two villages and an estimated 2000 Nisga'a perished when a nearby volcano erupted, spewing lava in a broad plain for 10 kilometres to the Nass River. The desolate landscape is the dominant feature of Nisga'a Memorial Lava Bed Provincial Park.

The Nass River rivals the Skeena and Fraser for significant salmon runs. These runs have been carefully studied by fisheries scientists employed by the Nisga'a. Innovative fish wheels have been installed on the river to accommodate research and food fish harvesting while still enabling the safe return of released fish. The substantial spring migrations of eulachon enabled the Nisga'a to create a thriving trade with other First Nations people. A coveted form of smelt, eulachon is particularly valued for its oil, which is rendered in large open vats. Since the dried fish are so oily that they sometimes burn, they are also often referred to as "candlefish."

The Nisga'a first petitioned for a land claim in 1887. In 1969, they began a legal process which, four years later, resulted in the Supreme Court of Canada acknowledging their pre-existing title to traditional lands. This landmark case helped define aboriginal rights when they became enshrined in the Canadian Constitution in 1982, and also led to the recognition of aboriginal title by the British Columbia government in 1991. The Nisga'a Treaty was ultimately ratified by the provincial and federal governments in 1999. The agreement defined ownership of land and awarded cash and resource rights to the Nisga'a who, in return, agreed to give up their exemption from taxation and to cease all further claims.

above *Nisga'a youngsters relax in New Aiyansh (also known as Gitlakdamiks)*

above *Nisga'a carver Alver Tait works on a
totem pole now erected in Gitwinksihlkw*

opposite *Young Nisga'a dancer whirls in ceremonial regalia*

above *Unusual drainage ponds formed when lava dammed the Tseax River in the mid-1700s*

above *Lava Lake cloaked by autumn mists*

above *The best way to reach the Salmon Glacier, located north of Stewart, is through Hyder, Alaska*

opposite *Lichen-encrusted lava flows of Nisga'a Memorial Lava Bed Provincial Park*

Haida Gwaii

The archipelago known as Haida Gwaii is shaped like a giant triangular wing floating in the Pacific Ocean. Inhabited by the Haida for thousands of years, these islands were named in 1787 for Queen Charlotte (wife of King George III) by Captain George Dixon of the British Navy. They include approximately 200 islands and islets extending over a 300-kilometre area. The closest is only 50 kilometres from the mainland coast. Just off Haida Gwaii's rocky western shores, the continental shelf drops steeply to the depths of the Pacific Ocean. The mixing of waters and weather make Cape St. James, at the southern tip, the windiest place in Canada, with sustained winds of over 175 kilometre per hour having been recorded.

Only the biggest of the islands, Graham and Moresby, are permanently inhabited. This was not always the case. In the past, at least 17 Haida villages were scattered throughout the archipelago. Large cedar-plank houses squarely faced the sea—the source of life. Intricately detailed totem poles lined the villages. The environment, both harsh and bountiful, fostered a strong and independent culture. Not linguistically related to mainland First Nation groups, some Haida claim that they, like their landmass, migrated from across the Pacific. The Haida were renowned for their construction of enormous seafaring canoes—some over 20 metres long—hewn from single, massive cedar trees. Sometimes, 40 men to a boat, they travelled from Alaska to Washington State, trading and raiding. Like most coastal groups, the Haida saw its population decimated by illness after European contact. Almost 9000 indigenous people were reduced to only 588 by 1915. Many villages were abandoned, with the survivors congregating in the villages of Masset and Skidegate.

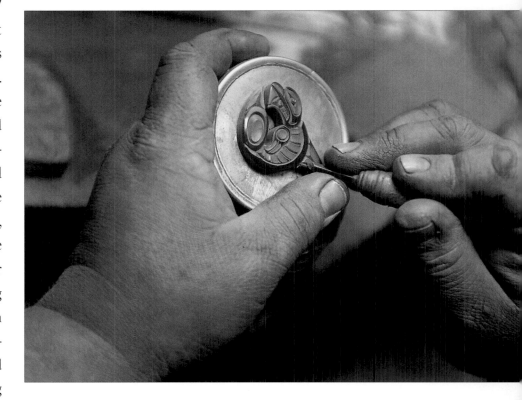

Today, however, the Haida population is rebounding. Their complex culture is reflected in a variety of sophisticated art pieces prized by collectors around the world. Miniature poles and carvings of polished black argillite—a fine slate found only on these islands—may be crafted solely by Haida artisans. The sale of raw argillite is forbidden. In 1985, images of Haida elders in ceremonial robes blockading logging crews on Lyell Island were telecast globally. These actions helped prompt formation of Gwaii Haanas National Park Reserve, co-managed by Parks Canada and the Council of the Haida Nation. The park features natural hot springs, abundant marine wildlife, abandoned village sites and Dolomite Narrows, a rich intertidal channel.

above *Haida artist Myles Edgars crafts an orca pendant in argillite*

opposite *Moss-cloaked frog detail on fallen totem pole, Nan Sdins (Ninstints) village*

above *House depression and moss-covered beams at T'anuu 'llnagaay (Tanu)*

opposite *Seaweed and algae at Gandll K'in Gwaayaay (Hot Spring Island)*

page 120 *The misty islands of Darwin Sound, Gwaii Haanas National Park Reserve*

page 121 *Tufted puffin near the southern tip of Haida Gwaii*

page 122 *Weathered mortuary poles at Nan Sdins (Ninstints) village, SGaang Gwaay (Anthony Island)*

page 123 *Haida watchman adorns contemporary monumental pole at Qay'llnagaay (Sealion Town) near Skidegate*

above *A black bear forages at low tide in Dolomite Narrows, Haida Gwaii*

opposite *A vibrant collection of intertidal life at Dolomite Narrows*

Acknowledgements

The making of this book has been a wonderful adventure. There are many people and organizations to which I am grateful for their contributions along the way.

I was fortunate to sail areas of the Great Bear Rainforest and Haida Gwaii with Mike Hobbis of Duen Adventures. His skillful seamanship, commitment to ecological and cultural education and graceful personality made our adventures all the richer. Eco-touring aboard a chartered yacht like the classic Duen, is one of the few means for people to experience the wonder of these remote coastal wilderness areas.

Many thanks to Dean Wyatt and his terrific staff at Knight Inlet Lodge for enabling myself and thousands of others to witness grizzlies in their own habitat, in a manner that is safe, thrilling and respectful of the animals.

There are many people I would like to thank and acknowledge: Tom Ellison and Jen Broom, for their hospitality aboard the beautiful sloop Ocean Light II in the Khutzeymateen (Tom has contributed greatly to public awareness of the coast, and bears in particular); Bernie Bowker, for piloting his Cessna 180 above tumultuous ocean, up steep-walled fiords and over the imposing ice-fields around Mt. Waddington, which enabled me to shoot many of the aerials in this book; the BC Ferry Corporation for the support in travelling the coast aboard the ferry fleet; Nikon Canada for the equipment loans; The Council of Haida Nations for allowing me to visit and photograph Gwaii Hanas; Tony Hunt and the Hunt Family Dancers; Raincoast Conservation Society; Western Canada Wilderness Committee, Friends of Clayoquot Sound, Greenpeace and the Sierra Club for their work towards creating a sustainable future; Doug Barron for knowledge and support with boats; Brian Henry for use of his Current Designs kayaks; Whistler Resort and Grouse Mountain for their support; the staff at Lens and Shutter for friendly and reliable service; Grant Faint for photographic inspiration and generosity, including the use of his cougar image in the Nature Highlights section on page 7; my publisher, Stephen Hutchings, for encouragement, expertise and commitment to quality; John Walls, also at Altitude Publishing, for sharing his enthusiasm about the book world. And, thanks to all the friends who have shared these special places with me.

Most of all I want to thank my wife Janice and my sons Dylan and Evan for their ongoing support and encouragement.

above *Tow Hill rising over Agate Beach, Naikoon Provincial Park, Graham Island*